W... ...... D I
S...   ...R?

WAYLAND

D0417167

WHY SHOULD I?

WHY SHOULD I Protect Nature?
WHY SHOULD I Recycle?
WHY SHOULD I Save Energy?
WHY SHOULD I Save Water?

Published in Great Britain in 2001 by Hodder Wayland,
an imprint of Hodder Children's Books
Reprinted in 2004, 2005, 2006(twice)
Reprinted in 2007(twice) and 2008 (twice)
© Copyright 2001 Wayland

Commissioning editor: Victoria Brooker
Editor: Liz Gogerly
Designer: Jean Wheeler
Digital Colour: Carl Gordon

Produced in association with WWF-UK.
WWF-UK registered charity number 1081247.
A company limited by guarantee number
4016725. Panda device © 1986 WWF ®
WWF registered trade mark owner.

Wayland,
338 Euston Road, London NW1 3BH
Wayland is a division of Hachette Children's Books,
an Hachette LIvre UK Company.
www.hachettelivre.co.uk

**British Library Cataloguing in
Publication Data**
Green, Jen, 1955 -
Why should I save water?
1.Water conservation - Juvenile literature
I.Title II.Gordon, Mike, 1948 - III.Save
water
333.9'116

ISBN-13: 978 0 7502 3689 8

Printed and bound in China

WHY SHOULD I SAVE WATER?

Written by Jen Green

Illustrated by Mike Gordon

WAYLAND

In my family, we all try to save water.

We used to waste a lot of water – until the hosepipe ban.

Before the ban, we all wasted water. We had a bath every day,

we always left the taps
running when we did
the washing up,

or when
we cleaned
our teeth.

One day, I was cleaning my bike when Kirsty from next door came round ...

9

Kirsty said that it hadn't
rained much lately ...

Kirsty said that if everyone wasted water there would be none left.

She said, 'Guess what will happen if everyone wastes water every day?'

'The water will run out, so there'll be none left for our gardens, or in the rivers and ponds.

'We'd all get very thirsty. People need water to live.

Animals need water to live too!

And what if the whole country ran out of water?'

'There would be no water
to wash with when we got dirty.'

20

So how can we save water?

Kirsty said there were lots of ways to save water.

'Showers are great and they use less water than a bath.

If we put a brick in the toilet, it will use less water when we flush.'

'It's easy to turn the tap off while we brush our teeth.

And we can save lots of water by doing full loads of washing.'

Kirsty was right! There are so many ways of saving water.

I thought of another good way to save water ...

Now my family uses less water.
It's good to know that we're doing
something to help.

And using less water means there's enough for everyone!

Notes for parents and teachers

Why Should I? and the National Curriculum

The *Why Should I?* series satisfies a number of requirements for the *Personal, Social and Health Education framework at Key Stage 1*. There are four titles about the environment in the series: *Why Should I Save Water?*, *Why Should I Save Energy?*, *Why Should I Protect Nature?* and *Why Should I Recycle?* Within the category of *Citizenship*, these books will help young readers to think about simple environmental issues, and other social and moral dilemmas they may come across in everyday life. Within the category of *Geography*, the books will help children to understand environmental change and how to recognize it in their own surroundings, and also help them to discover how their environment may be improved and sustained.

Why Should I Save Water? introduces the subject of water as a resource, and how it can be used either wastefully or wisely. The book introduces a number of simple tasks that children can do to help save water.

Suggestions for reading the book with children

As you read the book with children, you may find it helpful to stop and discuss issues as they come up in the text. Children might like to reread the story, taking on the role of different characters. Which character in the book mirrors their own attitudes to water more closely? How do their own ideas differ from those expressed in the book?

Discussing the subject of water may introduce children to a number of unfamiliar words, including standpipe, hosepipe ban, cistern, drought, environment, sewage, pollution. Make a list of all the new words and discuss what they mean.

Suggestions for follow-up activities

Discuss the various forms of water we come across in everyday life, including lakes and rivers, salt water in the sea, ice, and moisture in the air, that takes form in clouds which later shed rain. Introduce the subject of how water reaches our homes, and what happens to it when it runs down the drain. Water treatment works purify water so it is safe for us to drink, and sewage works treat dirty water so it doesn't pollute the natural world.

Encourage children to make a list of all the things we use water for, at home and also in the wider world. The book suggests a number of things that might happen if local water supplies run out. Children might have their own ideas about what might happen and how a water shortage would affect them. In the wider world, water is vital in farming and industry, and is also used to generate electricity. Children may already know that water is very scarce in some parts of the world. How do people in areas such as deserts survive with very little water? The book makes a number of suggestions about how water can be saved. What other ideas can children come up with for saving water?

Children might like to monitor how much water they use every day, using pages 12–13 as a starting point. As a general guide, a bucket contains roughly 10 litres of water. Taking a shower uses about 15 litres, as does washing dishes by hand. A dish washer uses 30 litres. An average bath uses 60–100 litres and a washing machine uses 120 litres. This information could be made into a chart, which should include how much water children drink. They could then work how much water they or their families use in a week. After implementing their water-saving ideas, how much water can they save?

Books to read

The Drop Goes Plop: A First Look at the Water Cycle
by Sam Godwin (Wayland, 1998).
A picture book which explains the water cycle.

How Green Are You? by David Bellamy
(Frances Lincoln, 1998)
A general introduction to the environment for young readers
that has many ideas about what we can all do to help save
the world.

Save the Planet: Stop Water Waste by Claire Llewellyn
(Chrysalis, 2005) A simple and fun introduction to
environmental issues. Teaches young children how to save
water, at home, at school and in their
local community.

I Can Help Save Our Water by V.
Smith (Franklin Watts, 2001)
Explains to young readers where
water comes from, how it gets to
them, and what happens to it
when they have used it.

Weather Around You: Rain by
Anita Ganeri (Wayland, 2004)
A beautiful first book on rain
including what happens when we
have too much or too little rain.